THE 132ND KENTUCKY DERBY
BARBARO

CHURCHILL DOWNS   MAY 6, 2006

To Keith and Dianne
Gretchen Jackson

Owners:	Lael Stables *(Roy & Gretchen Jackson)*
Trainer:	Michael Matz
Jockey:	Edgar Prado
Time:	2:01.36
Purse:	$2,213,200
Second:	Bluegrass Cat
Third:	Steppenwolfer

KENTUCKY DERBY 132
REVIEW

A MOONLIGHT PRESS BOOK

"I've never had a horse come to the Derby, let alone win it. It's a great feeling! Good horses make good riders, and good horses make good trainers."

THE HISTORY
132 REVIEW

*"This Kentucky Derby, whatever it is – a race, an emotion, a turbulence, an explosion –
is one of the most beautiful and violent and satisfying things I have ever experienced."*
— John Steinbeck, Nobel Prize-winning novelist —

The Kentucky Derby not only serves as the oldest continuously held sporting event in America, but is also one of the most prestigious races in the world. There is no other horse race that can match the tradition or excitement of the Kentucky Derby. The race that began in 1875 will celebrate its 133rd running at historic Churchill Downs on May 5, 2007.

Churchill Downs, founded by Colonel M. Lewis Clark, was originally named the Louisville Jockey Club and Driving Park Association. Clark developed his racetrack and the concept of stakes races such as the Derby, as a means to popularize racing and assist the Kentucky Thoroughbred breeding industry that had been devastated by the Civil War.

The first Kentucky Derby was held on Monday, May 17, 1875, and was won by a slight chestnut colt named Aristides. Owned by H. Price McGrath, Aristides was trained and ridden by African-Americans Ansel Williamson and Oliver Lewis, respectively. The total purse was $3,050 with a winner's share of $2,850.

Since that time a procession of Derby winners have added their names to the roster of Thoroughbred racing greats to have competed and won the coveted prize. Past champions such as War Admiral, Citation, Secretariat, and Seattle Slew have been joined by recent stars Silver Charm, Fusaichi Pegasus and Barbaro as winners of the famed "Run for the Roses."

Fascination with the Kentucky Derby takes in more than just Louisville and the Commonwealth of Kentucky, it captivates race fans from around the world. From its beginning, the race has been a spectacle to behold. A crowd of 10,000 witnessed the first Derby, with fans viewing the race from the infield aboard horses and carriages. In 2006, a crowd of 157,536, the second largest in Derby history, was on hand to witness the thrilling run by undefeated Barbaro in the 132nd running.

Owned by Roy and Gretchen Jackson's Lael Stables and trained by Michael Matz, Barbaro took command in the far turn and drew off under jockey Edgar Prado to win by an impressive 6 1/2-lengths. The margin was the most decisive since Assault's eight-length romp in 1946. Barbaro entered the record books as the sixth undefeated Derby champion. The Derby win was the first for both the Jacksons and Matz in just their first attempt, and the first for Prado in seven attempts.

The atmosphere at Churchill Downs on Kentucky Derby Day is like no other in the world of sports. Elegantly dressed ticket holders take in the day in their box seats while the spirited younger generation packs the infield. Magnificent Thoroughbreds nervously prance on the track, sensing the excitement of the day. These scenes come together under the time-honored Twin Spires of Churchill Downs to create an American classic – the Kentucky Derby.

The Kentucky Derby is Thoroughbred racing's ultimate dream. It's why countless horsemen spend hundreds of millions of dollars for unproven yearlings at the prestigious auctions. It's why trainers spend long hours – with early mornings and late nights – overseeing these prime Derby prospects at the barns. It's the Kentucky Derby and if you're lucky – and all things come together on the first Saturday in May – the dream just might come true.

San Francisco has the Golden Gate Bridge, Paris - the Eiffel Tower, Rome - the Coliseum, London - Big Ben. Certain cities throughout the world are instantly identified by particular structures, and the same is true of Louisville, which has the Twin Spires of Churchill Downs.

THE SPECTACLE
132 REVIEW

What is the Kentucky Derby? It is a horse race, fantastic party, glamorous fashion show and a chance to indulge in southern traditions such as sharing mint juleps with friends. The Derby is a spectacle steeped in tradition like none other in the world of sports as Thoroughbred racing captures the spotlight and all await the crowning of a new champion.

THE FASHION
132 REVIEW

The Kentucky Derby is truly one of America's greatest sporting and fashion events. Derby Day is a day to see and be seen, and at times fashion takes center stage as the action on the track becomes secondary to the scenes in the stands. And what lady would dare come to the Derby without a hat?

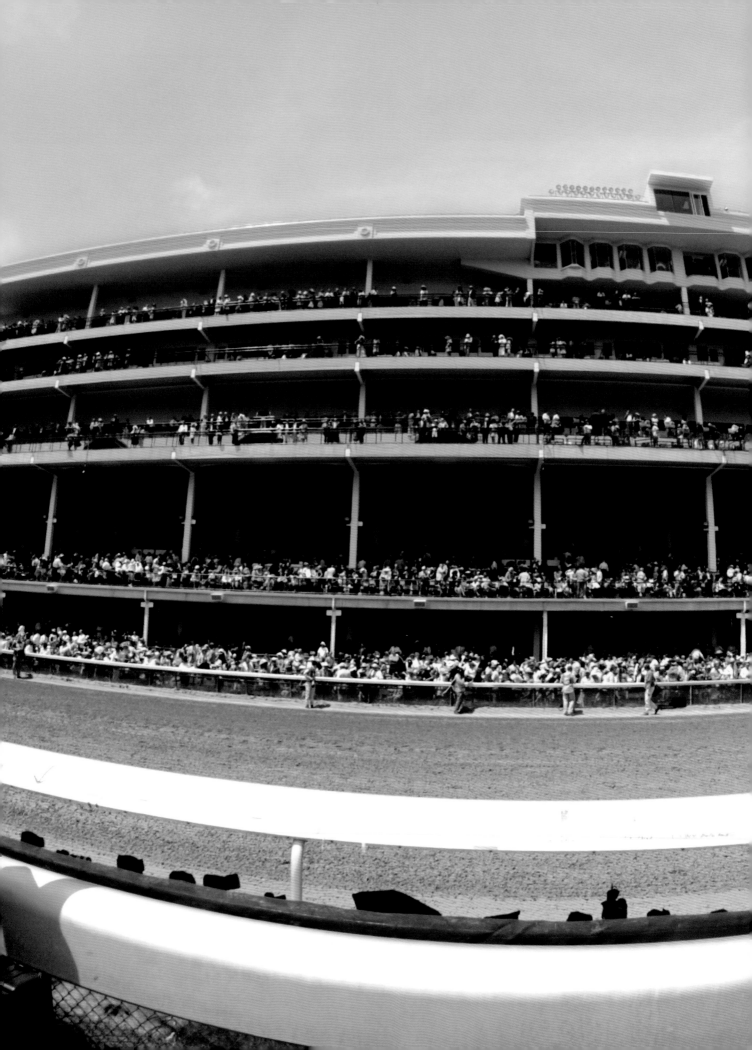

The $121 million renovation of Churchill Downs' clubhouse and grandstand is the most sweeping series of architectural changes at the track since 1895 when Churchill Downs' signature Twin Spires were added to the Louisville, Kentucky landmark. The new clubhouse and adjoining Jockey Club Suites combine all the charm and tradition of Churchill Downs with state-of-the-art racetrack comforts and conveniences.

THE STARS

132 REVIEW

is one of the Derby's most beloved traditions – celebrities. Throughout the rich history of the Derby an almost endless t of celebrities have found their way to the Bluegrass State to share in the fashion, food, mint juleps and overall party at is the Kentucky Derby. Beginning left to right, Top Row: Tennis great Serena Williams; Secretariat's Triple Crown key Ron Turcotte; actress Jennifer Love Hewitt. Middle Row: former Pittsburgh Steeler Lynn Swann; country music tist Travis Tritt, Motown legend Smokey Robinson. Bottom Row: Comedian Gilbert Gottfried; super-model trova Nemcova (opposite page also); rap artist Ludicris.

The call is made for the horsemen to begin the legendary walk from the relative tranquility of the stable area to the frenetic paddock, for saddling in front of a massive Derby Day crowd. Along the way, fans cheer their encouragement to Barbaro and his connections as they nervously make the trek to find their destiny and special place in Kentucky Derby history.

The years and weeks of preparation are complete. There is only one job left to do – make the march to the paddock to saddle for the Derby. The jockeys receive their final instructions and saddle up before they are led to the track. The scene is one of the high points of the Derby spectacle as crowds fill the paddock area to catch a glimpse of the Derby contenders. Trainer Michael Matz made it a family experience when he shared the special moment with his son.

All cameras are focused on the 20 Derby contenders, the cream of a foal crop of nearly 34,000, who are fortunate enough to have their chance to wear the famed garland of roses as the Kentucky Derby winner. In anticipation of the annual running of the world's most famous race, everyone becomes a captivated fan - from former NBA star and broadcaster John Salley, above, to the youngest supporters in the Barbaro camp, left. Note the back of the blue cap of winning jockey Edgar Prado, borrowed from fellow rider Cornelio Velasquez for the big race.

THE POST PARADE
132 REVIEW

Each year as the bugler takes his position above the Winner's Circle for the official "Call to Post," the Thoroughbreds anxiously prance onto the track and the University of Louisville Marching Band plays *My Old Kentucky Home*. It is the moment that the crowd has anticipated all day, and for every Derby owner, trainer, and jockey, it is the moment they have awaited their entire lives.

Some contenders merely become Kentucky Derby footnotes, while others make Derby history. Twenty horses went to the post for the 132nd Run for the Roses accompanied by outriders featuring the logo of presenting sponsor, Louisville based Yum! Brands. Yum! is better known as the parent company for fast food giants KFC, Taco Bell, Long John Silvers, Pizza Hut, and A&W.

Lael Stable owners Roy and Gretchen Jackson created their own history as they became the first owners in Derby history to start two undefeated horses in the "Run for the Roses." Barbaro, above, was the second choice in the wagering, while his stablemate Showing Up, middle, was dismissed at 26-1, and finished respectably in sixth place after tiring in the stretch.

Sweetnorthernsaint, bottom, earned his own Derby footnote, as the 5-1 wagering favorite, but finished in seventh place.

The plans and preparations have all been made – the breeding, the training, the prep-races, and the selection of the perfect rider that will give the perfect ride. The gates spring open and the moment is at hand. It will take just over two minutes to see if even the best laid plans will stand the challenge of the 1-1/4-mile Kentucky Derby.

"He stumbled coming out of the gate a little bit and after that,
he just took hold and went right with the leaders."
— Edgar Prado, Jockey

As if he were flying, a high-stepping Barbaro seemed airborne as he charged down the stretch for the first time with jockey Edgar Prado. Many of the veteran Kentucky Derby photographers commented that they had never photographed a horse whose unique stride allowed him to stay aloft for as long a period as Barbaro.

As the field neared the first turn, Barbaro tucked in behind the leaders alongside stablemate Showing Up. With the backdrop of the tote board monitor showing the action, the horses and their jockeys battled for strategic position.

Jockey Edgar Prado, on a relaxed and patient Barbaro, maintained perfect early position near the lead moving into the first turn in the Kentucky Derby.

As the field entered the backstretch, Prado placed Barbaro fourth on the outside as they passed a throng of fans and the barn that once housed 1992 Kentucky Derby winner Lil E. Tee. Note the sign paying tribute to his victory.

The pivotal moment...taking command around the turn and getting the lead, Barbaro and Prado were in perfect form as the jockey called on his horse and the handsome bay colt responded like an ultimate professional. Barbaro quickly charged from fourth to first in the course of the turn and held a three-length advantage at the top of the stretch.

49

*"My horse was doing everything so easy, I was very confident.
It was just a matter of time when I could turn him loose
and you see what happened when I did!"*
— Edgar Prado, Jockey

With the finish in sight, Barbaro coasted home in front of a captivated crowd of 157,536, including the annual ROTC Color Guard stationed along the home stretch.

Nearing the finish, Barbaro flashed by the Churchill Downs tote board en route to his smashing victory. Denoted at the generous odds of 6-1, he proved a betting bargain and rewarded his backers with a $14.00 payoff for a $2.00 win ticket.

"A dream come true." – Roy Jackson, Owner

Barbaro crossed the wire with a convincing 6 1/2-length win, adding his name to the Derby record book with these marks: sixth undefeated horse to win the Run for the Roses following Regret (1915), Morvich (1922), Majestic Prince (1969), Seattle Slew (1977), and Smarty Jones (2004); fifth largest win margin in history, and largest since Assault in 1946; and 13th fastest time of 2:01.36.

"My mother passed away on January 19 and the following big race I won was the Florida Derby, and I dedicated that to my mother and this one too...every race that I've won, I am thinking of her."

– Edgar Prado, Jockey

"I'm very excited and very happy, and especially for Mr. Matz and Mr. and Mrs. Jackson and all of the people that came here to enjoy the show. I'm very glad it was a beautiful show."

— Edgar Prado, Jockey

Temperatures on Derby Day climbed to nearly 70 degrees and gave jockey Edgar Prado a good reason to cool off Barbaro with a dousing from his water bottle.

"For some reason, this horse has given us terrific confidence all along...I don't know why I was so positive about it except to look at him, see him, and I thought he's going to out in a strong performance. And what a job he did."

— Gretchen Jackson, Owner

As is the tradition, many owners lead their horses into the Winner's Circle following victory. In front of a television audience of millions, owner Gretchen Jackson led Barbaro into the Winner's Circle as her husband, Roy, awaited the pair for the photograph and presentation.

"We've been in racing for a long time. You always dream about getting to the Kentucky Derby. Just getting here was something really special for us, and to win it is...I haven't come up with the words to express it right now."

— Roy Jackson, Owner

"What can I say? Everybody saw it, so they know what he did...we've never missed anything in his training, never wavered one bit from our plan that my assistant and I wanted to do...looks like we made the right plan."
— Michael Matz, Trainer

As the Derby trophy glistened in the Kentucky sunlight, Jackson, Matz, and Prado held the coveted 14-karat gold cup overhead celebrating Barbaro's thrilling victory.

Roy Jackson's comments in the Kentucky Derby post race interview summed up the roller-coaster ride that he and his wife Gretchen had experienced – *"I think all of you know that have followed racing, you really have your ups and downs. And we just are enjoying it, I don't know why these circumstances have happened, but we're really enjoying it."*

THE CHAMPION
132 REVIEW

OWNERS – Roy and Gretchen Jackson - Lael Stables

For owners Roy and Gretchen Jackson who race under the Lael Stable name, Saturday, May 6, 2006, was not only Derby Day, it was their dream day. Through 47 years of marriage the Jacksons have shared in dreams that have come and gone. Their racing experience began with a modest $7,500 yearling purchase. Success did not come initially, but they persevered and in 1978 purchased their 190-acre Lael Farm in West Grove, Pennsylvania. This would serve as a base for their Thoroughbred breeding and racing, a place where dreams could be created, nurtured and sent out to glory.

Roy, a graduate of Pennsylvania University, brought a background in baseball to his racing operations. A president of two minor league baseball teams – the Toros (Tuscon, AZ) and the Pirates (York, PA), Roy and two associates began Convest Incorporated in 1982, a firm representing professional baseball players. Jackson eventually sold the company in 2001 to devote his interest to racing.

The stage was set to make their dreams come true when the Jacksons decided to upgrade their racing stock with female runners to build their broodmare band. One of these purchases was La Ville Rouge, the dam of Barbaro. La Ville Rouge in English means "The Red Town." Little did the Jacksons know that this special broodmare would someday bring them Derby glory and allow them to paint the racing world red.

The 132nd Kentucky Derby played out like a storybook for the Jacksons. Even before Barbaro's sensational 6 1/2 -length win, the Jackson's secured their spot in Derby history when they became the first owners in Derby history to send two undefeated starters into the race. Barbaro, their handsome homebred son of Dynaformer, came into the race with a spotless five race win streak. Showing Up, a $60,000 purchase who was unraced as a two year-old, had three sharp victories to his credit. With this dynamic duo The Jacksons were winners even before Barbaro crossed the wire at Churchill Downs.

TRAINER – Michael Matz

Hard work and diligence are trademarks for the success that Michael Matz has achieved in the world of equine sports. Long before his fame as trainer of Kentucky Derby winner Barbaro, Matz served as an accomplished horseman. A highly rated rider, Matz competed in three Olympic Games as a member of the U.S. equestrian team. His efforts were rewarded in 1996 as he earned the silver medal and was chosen to carry the American flag in the Atlanta Summer Olympics.

The pressures that horsemen face while competing in the Kentucky Derby are not generally covered by the media. Trainers face an endless number of decisions while conditioning the horses which have been entrusted to them. In 1989, Matz was faced with circumstances and pressures unlike any faced by most horsemen. His decision making would save the lives of three children following a tragic jetliner crash in Sioux City, Iowa. While the fuselage was burning Matz quickly gathered up the children ages, 9, 12 and 14 and led them to safety. The children are all grown now but still follow the career of Matz and were at Churchill Downs on Derby Day to watch Michael achieve his greatest equine glory – a win in the Kentucky Derby.

Michael's unconventional training strategy would be the subject of much discussion prior to the 132nd Kentucky Derby. Leading up to the race Matz felt the sting of criticism as he was questioned about the five-week layoff Barbaro was given from his Florida Derby win to the Kentucky Derby. Only one other Derby winner in modern history (Needles) had been successful in taking that approach and that was fifty years earlier. Yet Matz's training goal was not only to have a horse ready to win the Kentucky Derby, but also one that was fresh enough to take on all the rigors of the Triple Crown. Matz was emphatically rewarded for his patient handling of Barbaro with a breathtaking 6 1/2-length Kentucky Derby victory.

JOCKEY – Edgar Prado

Jockey Edgar Prado has ridden for 23 years in a career that includes over 5,000 wins, but until he charged across the wire aboard Barbaro in the 132nd Kentucky Derby his career was not complete. Most riders will admit that it's not really the number of wins that defines their careers. More important to jockeys are wins in the biggest races, and among the big wins, the Kentucky Derby is the biggest win of them all.

Prado learned the riding profession in his native Peru and tallied his first win in 1983. The following year he was Peru's leading rider. In 1986 he made the leap of faith and ventured to the United States in search of the bigger races and lucrative earnings. His journey would lead him to Miami's Calder Race Course, followed by New England and Maryland. It was in Maryland that he became a national force and by 1997 he was the leading rider in America. Then came the move to the prestigious New York racing circuit – a move that was quickly rewarded as he earned his first New York title at Belmont in 2000. As with all top riders, Prado has traveled throughout North America in search of racing's greatest prizes piloting the most talented horses.

The quest for the Kentucky Derby has brought Prado to Louisville every year since 2000. In his first attempt, he crossed the wire a disappointing 17th on Commendable in a field of 19. Since that time Edgar has twice experienced the thrill of being a top contender, but neither time did he taste victory. In 2002 Prado had the mount on favored Harlan's Holiday but finished seventh. The following year, Edgar made the turn for home with a half-length advantage aboard Peace Rules and seemed poised to etch his name to the roster of esteemed Derby winners, but faded in the stretch to finish third.

Barbaro was special, and Prado knew he was well-armed heading into the Derby. The jockey and horse had been teamed by trainer Michael Matz who chose Prado to ride the colt as he entered his three year-old campaign. They had met the challenges marked out by Matz's Derby prep campaign, reeling off three wins in Florida beginning with the Tropical Park Derby held on New Year's Day, followed by the Holy Bull Stakes and finally the Florida Derby.

The Derby would be just the fourth time that Prado climbed aboard Barbaro in competition. The two performed that day as if they were one. Early on, Prado placed Barbaro on the outside away from the traffic problems just off the rail. Stalking the leaders in fourth position down the backstretch, Prado made the decision to move as they approached the turn and Barbaro complied in thrilling fashion. The Peruvian jockey and his Kentucky-bred Thoroughbred were in unison as they charged into the lead at the top of the stretch and quickly opened up a three-length lead and finally drew away to a 6 1/2-length win.

The Derby win was 23 years in the making for Prado, but proved to be the win of a lifetime.

THE WINNER'S PEDIGREE AND CAREER HIGHLIGHTS

			Hail to Reason
	Dynaformer	Roberto	Bramalea
		Andover Way	His Majesty
Barbaro			On the Trail
Dark bay/brown colt		Carson City	Mr. Prospector
	La Ville Rouge		Blushing Promise
		La Reine Rouge	King's Bishop
			Silver Betsy

YEAR	AGE	STS.	1ST	2ND	3RD	EARNINGS
2005	2	2	2	0	0	$99,000
2006	3	5	4	0	0	$2,203,200
TOTALS		7	6	0	0	$2,302,200

At 2 Years	WON	Laurel Futurity, Maiden on First Attempt
At 3 Years	WON	Kentucky Derby, Florida Derby, Holy Bull, Tropical Park Derby
	DNF	Preakness

Horse	M/Eq	Wt.	PP	1/4	1/2	3/4	MILE	STR.	FIN.	Jockey	Owner	Odds To $1
Barbaro	L	126	8	5 1/2	4 1-1/2	4 1/2	1 3	1 4	1 6-1/2	E.S. Prado	Lael Stables	6.10
Bluegrass Cat	L	126	13	8 1/2	5 1/2	6 1/2	3 1	2 1/2	2 2	R.A. Dominguez	WinStar Farm, LLC.	30.00
Steppenwolfer	L	126	2	18 1/2	13 hd	11 1/2	6 hd	5 1	3 1	R.J. Albarado	Robert and Lawana Low	16.30
Jazil (dh)	L	126	1	20	20	19 1/2	17 2	6 1	4	F. Jara	Shadwell Farm, LLC.	24.20
Brother Derek (dh)	L	126	18	9 1-1/2	9 1/2	14 1/2	10 hd	7 1/2	4 1/2	A. Solis	Cecil N. Peacock	7.70
Showing Up	L	126	6	4 hd	3 hd	3 hd	2 hd	3 1-1/2	6 3	C. Valesquez	Lael Stables	26.20
Sweetnorthernsaint	Lb	126	11	12 1	11 1	5 1/2	4 hd	4 hd	7 1	K.J. Desormeaux	Joseph J. Balsamo & Ted Theos	5.50
Deputy Glitters	L	126	14	13 1	15 1/2	16 1/2	9 1	10 1	8 1-1/4	J. Lezcano	Joseph LaCombe Stables, Inc.	60.60
Point Determined	Lb	126	5	11 1/2	10 hd	7 1	7 hd	8 1/2	9 hd	R. Bejarano	The Robert & Beverly Lewis Estate	9.40
Seaside Retreat	L	126	15	7 hd	7 1-1/2	10 1/2	15 hd	9 hd	10 4-1/2	P. Husbands	William S. Farish, Jr.	52.50
Storm Treasure	L	126	19	19 2-1/2	18 2	13 hd	12 hd	11 1/2	11 1-3/4	D.R. Flores	Mike McCarty	51.90
Lawyer Ron	L	126	17	6 1/2	8 1/2	9 hd	8 1/2	12 1-1/2	12 no	J. McKee	Estate of James T. Hines, Jr.	10.20
Cause to Believe	L	126	16	15 1/2	19 2	20	18 4	17 2	13 3	R.A. Baze	Peter Redekop Ltd. & Peter Abruzzo	25.90
Flashy Bull	L	126	20	16 1	17 hd	17 1	14 1/2	15 1	14 2-1/2	M.E. Smith	West Point Thoroughbreds, LLC	43.00
Private Vow	L	126	12	17 1/2	16 1/2	12 1/2	11 1/2	14 1-1/2	15 2-3/4	S.X. Bridgmohan	Mike McCarty	40.50
Sinister Minister	Lb	126	4	2 1-1/2	2 2	2 1-1/2	5 1	13 1-1/2	16 1-1/2	V. Espinoza	Lanni Fam Tr&Mercedes St.&Schiappa	9.70
Bob and John	Lb	126	7	14 1/2	12 1	8 hd	16 1/2	16 1/2	17 nk	G.K. Gomez	Stonerside Stable	12.90
A. P. Warrior	L	126	10	10 1/2	14 1	18 1/2	19 5	19 5	18 1-1/2	C.S. Nakatani	Stan E. Fulton	14.10
Sharp Humor	L	126	9	3 1/2	6 hd	15 1-1/2	20	20	19 7-1/2	M. Guidry	Purdedel Stable	30.10
Keyed Entry	L	126	3	1 hd	1 2	1 1-1/2	13 hd	18 2-1/2	20	P.A. Valenzuela	Starlight St. & Saylor & Lucarelli	28.80

Time: :22³, :46,1:10⁴, 1:37, 2:01¹ (:22.63,:46.07, 1:10.88, 1:37.02, 2:01.36). Track Fast. OFF at 6:15 EDT. Start good for all but BARBARO. Won driving.

Program #		Win	Place	Show	$2 Exacta (8-13)	$2 Trifecta (8-13-2)	$1 Superfecta (8-13-2-1)
8	Barbaro	$14.20	$8.00	$6.00	$587.00	$11,418.40	$84,860.40
13	Bluegrass Cat		$28.40	$15.40			$1 Superfecta (8-13-2-18)
2	Steppenwolfer			$7.80			$59,839.00

Winner - Dk. b or b. c, (Apr), by Dynaformer - La Ville Rouge, by Carson City. Trainer Matz Michael R. Bred by Mr. & Mrs. M Roy Jackson (Ky).
$2,213,200- gross value and $90,000 Gold Cup. Net to winner $1,453,200; second $400,000; third $200,000; fourth $80,000; fourth $80,000 .

BARBARO stumbled at the start, came up runing and leaned in soon after bumping with BOB AND JOHN placing him in tight, raced under light restraint while between horses early, continued five or six wide around the first turn and into the backstretch, raced to the leaders under his own power midway on the far turn, reached the front at the five-sixteenths pole, accelerated quickly to a clear advantage approaching the stretch while angling near the inside, then drew off under strong hand urging as much the best. BLUEGRASS CAT, never far back, maneuvered nicely between foes to reach the rail entering the first turn, followed BARBARO while just inside that one on the backstretch, angled outside the winner nearing the final quarter, then couldn't menace at the end while clearly second best. STEPPENWOLFER, bumped after the start by KEYED ENTRY and forced in, saved ground in hand, rallied between horses three or four wide on the far turn, lacked room at the five-sixteenths pole, worked his way out six wide when straightened into the stretch to make his run, loomed a threat through the upper stretch, then failed to sustain his bid while drifting out slightly. JAZIL swerved in at the start, was unhurried while outrun for six furlongs, continued to save ground while rallying along the rail on the far turn, angled out between foes four wide, when entering the upper stretch to make a serious bid but failed to sustain his effort while dead heating with BROTHER DEREK for fourth. BROTHER DEREK worked his way in six wide by the first turn, moved out wider when the field bunched nearing the end of the backstretch where he was steadied twice, fanned out nine abreast when making a run into the upper stretch, but came up empty while finishing even with JAZIL for fourth. SHOWING UP bobbled at the break, came out bumping with BOB AND JOHN, gained a forward position near the inside, went along under careful handling, raced between foes four wide nearing the final quarter, was just off the winner briefly when entering the stretch and flattened out in the drive. SWEETNORTHERNSAINT, steadied when bumped at the start by A.P. WARRIOR and forced out on PRIVATE VOW, was steadied again under the wire the first time in tight quarters, worked his way between foes around the first turn, angled inside on the backstretch, boldly came through close quarters along the rail at the five-sixteenths pole, but faltered when straightened for the drive. DEPUTY GLITTERS, outrun five wide into the backstretch, inched forward around the far turn, came out eleven wide for the drive, leaned in and bumped SEASIDE RETREAT at the furlong grounds, then lacked a further response. POINT DETERMINED, bobbled lightly at the start, was well placed near the inside from the outset, moved between horses five wide into the lane, came out and bumped with SEASIDE RETREAT at the eight pole and was finished. SEASIDE RETREAT, unhurried and six wide, reached striking distance on the far turn, came out wider entering the stretch, was bumped from both sides at the eight pole and had no further account. STORM TREASURE, steadied behind horses nearing the first turn, made a mild move between rivals approaching the final quarter but failed to continue. LAWYER RON, well placed early, raced between foes around the the first turn, was steadied entering the backstretch, continued to within striking distance until the stretch and tired. CAUSE TO BELIEVE never reached contention. FLASHY BULL broke awkwardly and raced wide most of the way. PRIVATE VOW, sluggish to start, was bumped soon after by SWEETNORTHERNSAINT and steadied, then never was a factor. SINISTER MINISTER vied for the lead soon after start while battling outside of KEYED ENTRY, surrendered the advantage to that one just before the opening quarter expired, tracked KEYED ENTRY to the far turn, briefly gained the lead between calls approaching the stretch, lost it to the winner after several strides and faded. BOB AND JOHN, bumped at the start by SHOWING UP, then steadied soon after and bumped again when BARBARO leaned in, was finished after seven furlongs. A.P. Warrior came out at the start bumping SWEETNORTHERNSAINT, then was finished early. SHARP HUMOR came out after the start bumping A.P. Warrior, faded after a half, bore out midway on the second turn and wasn't abused in the drive. KEYED ENTRY leaned in at the start bumping STEPPENWOLFER, went up inside SINISTER MINISTER to fight for the lead, gained a slight edge after going a quarter, was clear on the first turn, showed the way to the far turn and gave way readily after seven furlongs.
440 nominations.
Medication: L-lasix.

EPILOGUE
132 REVIEW

Perfection is the quality mark that all craftsmen and professionals struggle to obtain. On May 6, 2006, perfection was embodied by a three year-old Thoroughbred named Barbaro. The dreams of Derby perfection were realized by owners Roy and Gretchen Jackson who arranged the breeding that would produce this stunning Derby champion. The expert conditioning by trainer Michael Matz provided a dominating 6 1/2-length win over the best three year-olds in the world. And finally, after over 5,000 wins, Jockey Edgar Prado would have his own view of perfection from atop a Derby champion as he cruised through a superb 1 1/4 mile journey in 2:01.36.

Thoroughbred racing had a new hero and many race fans anticipated that Barbaro could be the first Triple Crown champion since Affirmed's sweep in 1978. The Preakness, the second leg in the Triple Crown held at Baltimore's Pimlico Race Course, awaited Barbaro. A field of nine including the Derby champ entered the race. Barbaro drew post position six and as the odds-on favorite, faced Derby veterans Sweetnorthernsaint and Brother Derek as well as six new challengers.

Preakness day brought excitement and anticipation as the crowd and a national television audience looked forward to what would surely be another stunning performance. Barbaro, sharp and focused, awaited the start but grew impatient and broke through the gate and was quickly brought to a halt by jockey Edgar Prado. Before the stunned crowd, Barbaro was reloaded and once again poised for the start. The bell rang, the gates sprung open with a crash and the field charged down the track, but this was not a normal start for Barbaro. Within the first few strides, Prado sensed that his champion had injured himself and struggled to pull up the distressed colt, eliminating him from the competition.

The dream had ended and wins and losses were no longer a concern for the pride of the Lael Stable. Barbaro had fractured three bones in and around the ankle of his right hind leg. He was loaded into an equine ambulance and rushed to the University of Pennsylvania's New Bolton Center in Kennett Square, Pa.

Just as Barbaro had faced the challenges on the track, he now faced a new set of obstacles. His initial rounds of surgery were compromised when a severe case of the life-threatening hoof disease laminitis attacked the champion. His former racing team was replaced by a team of veterinarians, headed by Dr. Dean Richardson, head of surgery at the New Bolton Center. Through all of the surgery and complications, Barbaro proved to be the perfect patient, showing all the strength and intelligence he exhibited on the track. As 2006 comes to an end, the courageous colt that once dominated on the track faces a slow period of recovery. It is this strong will and heart of a champion that have endeared Barbaro to countless fans in America and around the world. The fans now cheer his medical victories as greatly as they once cheered his achievements on the track.

A record of six wins from seven races is a small footnote that will never truly explain the spirit of Barbaro – the Champion of the 132nd Kentucky Derby, May 6, 2006.

Kentucky Derby: 132 Review
©2006 Moonlight Press
All Rights Reserved.

ISBN 9780970963949
Library of Congress Control Number 2006935702

Printed in the United States.

Executive Editor: Leonard Lusky
Creative Director: Cary Meyer
Administrative Assistant: Kelli Garvey
Copy: Tony Terry, *Churchill Downs, Director of Publicity*
Copy Editor: Julie Koenig Loignon, *Churchill Downs Inc., Vice President of Communications*

Contact Information

Moonlight Press
P.O. Box 4865
Louisville, Kentucky 40204

For more information, including orders, volume discounts and corporate customization, call (502) 473-1036 or email at derbyreview@secretariat.com.

Moonlight Press would like to thank Angie Fleitz, Tobey Roush, Laura Botner, Mike Doctrow, Peggy Gdovka, Gretchen and Roy Jackson and the entire Barbaro family and friends.

A portion of the proceeds from the sale of this book will benefit the Laminitis Fund at the University of Pennsylvania School of Veterinary Medicine's New Bolton Center.

Photographers
John Chan
Pam Davis
Larry Foster
Bruce Fratto
Phil Groshong
Dave Hooker
John Sattler
Ray Schuhmann
Tom Schuhmann
Al Wollerton
Antz Yent Wettig
Jon Clark Wettig
Christine Zalewa
Don Zalewa

Director of Photography: Ray Schuhmann
Derby Archivist: Ann Tatum
Art Director: Tim Pitts

email: DerbyArchives@Kinetic.Distillery.com
Website: www.DerbyArchives.com

Contact Information

Kinetic Corporation
200 Distillery Commons, Suite 200
Louisville, KY 40206-1990
502.719.9500 Phone
502.719.9509 Fax

All of the imagery is from the Official Kentucky Derby Photographic Archives. Kinetic has been the Official Photographer and Archivist for the Kentucky Derby for over 50 years.

Individual print orders of any of these images, or any previous years Derby, are available by calling the Kentucky Derby Photo Archivist at 502.719.9500 or placing an order on-line at the above website address. For best rates enter "KD132mp" in the Promotion Code box. Commercial and editorial use also available, permission must be granted.